Vocabulary ...

Fantastic Ants

Elizabeth Bennett

SCHOLASTIC INC.

NEW YORK • TORONTO • LONDON • AUCKLAND • SYDNEY
MEXICO CITY • NEW DELHI • HONG KONG • BUENOS AIRES

ISBN-13: 978-0-545-00737-5 / ISBN-10: 0-545-00737-2

Photos Credits:

Cover: © Gail Shumway/Getty Images; title page: © Neil Lucas/Nature Picture Library; contents page, from top: © Scott Smith/Corbis, © Fabio Colombini/Animals Animals, © James Robinson/Animals Animals, © Prema Photos/Nature Picture Library; page 4: © Scott Smith/Corbis; page 5, top left: © Mark Moffett/ Minden Pictures; page 5, top right: © Michael and Patricia Fogden/Minden Pictures; page 5, bottom left: © Duncan Mcewan/NPL/Minden Pictures; page 5, bottom right: © Mark Moffett/Minden Pictures; page 6: © George B. Diebold/Corbis; page 7: © Jim Zuckerman/Corbis; page 8: © Fabio Colombini/Animals Animals; page 9, top left: © Frans Lanting/Minden Pictures; page 9, top right: © Fritz Prenzel/Animals Animals; page 9, bottom left: © Konrad Wothe/Minden Pictures; page 10: © Mark Moffett/Minden Pictures; page 11: © Mark Moffett/Minden Pictures; page 12: Jim McMahon; page 13: © Doug Cheeseman/Peter Arnold Inc.; page 13, inset: © Kim Taylor; page 14, top left: © Mark Moffett/Minden Pictures; page 14, top right: © Piotr Naskrecki/Minden Pictures; page 14, bottom left: © Stephen Dalton/ Minden Pictures; page 14, bottom right: © James Robinson/Animals Animals; page 15, top left: © Greg Harold/Auscape/Minden Pictures; page 15, top right: © Piotr Naskrecki/Minden Pictures; page 15, bottom left: © Babs and Bert Wells/OSF/Animals Animals; page 15, bottom right: © James Robinson/Animals Animals; page 16, both: © Mark Moffett/Minden Pictures; page 17: © Scott W. Smith/Animals Animals; page 18: © Prema Photos/Nature Picture Library; page 19: © Dietmar Nill/Nature Picture Library; page 20: © Reg Morrison/Auscape/Minden Pictures; page 21: © Konrad Wothe/Minden Pictures; page 21, inset: © Mark Moffett/Minden Pictures; page 22: © David M. Dennis/Animals Animals; page 23: © Greg Harold/ Auscape/Minden Pictures; page 24: © Kim Taylor/Minden Pictures; backcover: © James Robinson/ Animals Animals.

Photo research by Dwayne Howard
Design by Holly Grundon

12 11 10 9 8 7 6 5 4 3 2 8 9 10 11 12 13/0

Printed in the U.S.A.
First printing, March 2008

Contents

Chapter 1

All About Ants

Ants may be tiny. But they are also fantastic! This book will tell you all about them.

bee

butterfly

ladybug

ant

Ants are insects. They have three body parts and six legs, just like these other insects.

Ant Parts

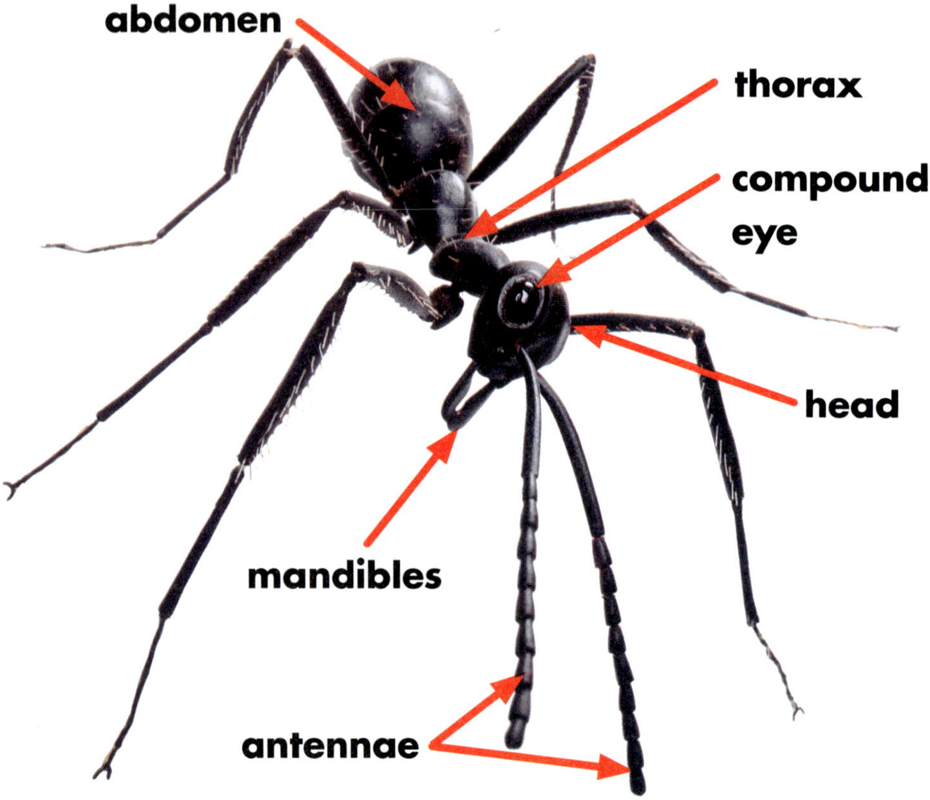

Ants have strong jaws called **mandibles**. They also have **antennae**, which they use to smell, taste, and touch.

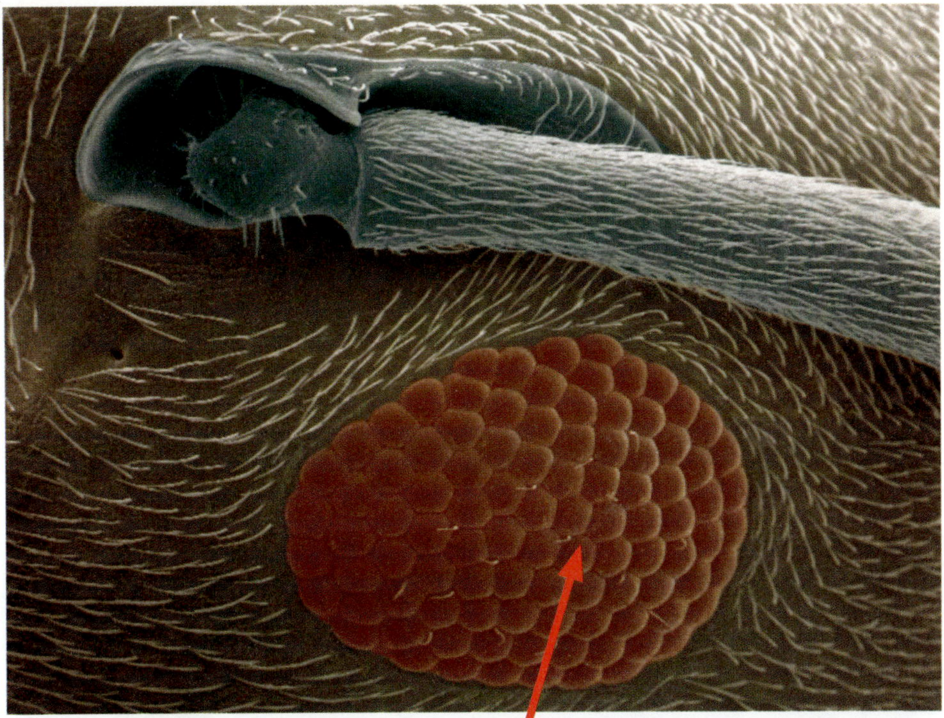

Close Up!

The compound eye of an ant looks like this. It is made up of lots of tiny lenses.

Most kinds of ants have five eyes. They have three simple eyes to see light. They have two big **compound eyes** to see all around.

Chapter 2

Ant Colonies

This is an anthill.

Ants are **social insects**. That means they live in groups and help one another to survive. You have probably seen an anthill like this.

sand

mud

pine needles

Fast Fact

Anthills are filled with lots of tunnels and rooms.

But did you know that anthills are also made of dried mud and pine needles? More than one million ants can live in a single hill!

Fast Fact

A queen ant can lay millions of eggs in her lifetime.

An ant group is called a **colony**. A colony is a busy place! It has one queen ant. She is the biggest ant in the colony. Her job is to lay all of the eggs.

Leafcutter ants bring plants back to their nest.

List

Worker Ant Jobs

- collect food
- build and repair nest
- protect colony
- feed other ants
- care for queen
- care for young

An ant colony has thousands of worker ants. Different ones have different jobs. Some collect food. Some build nests. Some take care of the teeny baby ants.

Chapter 3

Ants, Ants, Ants!

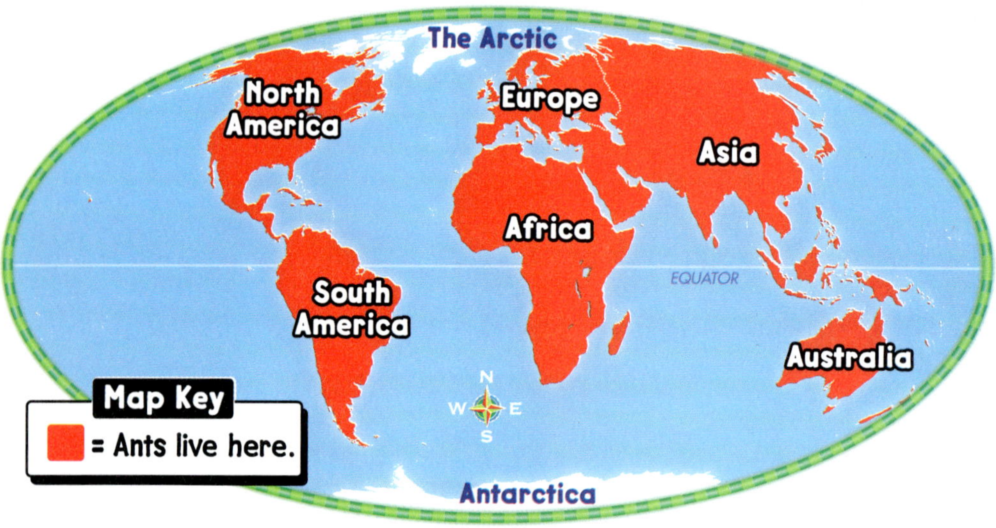

Ants live all over the world. They live almost everywhere except the Arctic and Antarctica. Why? Those places are too cold for ants to survive.

Millions of driver ants march across the land.

Fast Fact

A male driver ant is this size in real life.

There are more than 8,000 kinds of ants in the world. Which are the largest? The answer is driver ants. Some male driver ants grow to be over an inch long!

wood ant

bullet ant

black garden ant

red fire ant

Here are eight other kinds of ants. Take a look.

pink-faced green ant

acacia ant

bulldog ant

red carpenter ant

How are these ants alike? How are they different?

This harvester ant likes to eat seeds.

This trapjaw ant likes to eat insects.

Ants eat a lot of things. Some munch on plants and seeds. Some munch on other insects.

List

Ant Menu

- plants
- seeds
- pollen
- insects
- tree sap
- fruit
- candy
- spilled juice

Ants eat fruit and candy, too. Why? These sweet treats are loaded with sugar, which gives them energy!

Chapter 4

Teamwork Time

weaver ants

It is amazing what ants can do when they **cooperate**. Weaver ants sew leaves together to make cozy nests.

wood ants

Wood ants use teamwork to attack a much bigger insect. Later, this wasp will be dinner!

Fast Fact

Honeypot ants hang upside down like bats!

Honeypot ants store nectar in their huge abdomens. When food is **scarce**, they will share the nectar with their fellow ants.

Leafcutter ants use their powerful jaws to cut leaves.

Leafcutter ants work together to cut leaves from plants. Then, they carry the leaves back to their nest.

Fast Fact

If a man could lift 20 times his body weight, he could lift a car!

Leafcutter ants are super strong. They can lift leaves that weigh 20 times their own weight. Wow! Aren't ants fantastic?

Glossary

antennae (an-**ten**-ee): feelers on an insect's head

colony (**kol**-uh-nee): a large group of insects that live and work together

compound eye (**kom**-pound **eye**): an eye made up of many tiny, simple eyes that work together

cooperate (koh-**op**-uh-rate): to work together

lenses (**lenz**-uz): the clear part of eyes that focuses light

mandibles (**man**-duh-buhlz): a pair of strong jaws

scarce (**skairss**): hard to find or rare

social insect (**soh**-shuhl in-sekt): insects that live and work together

stun (**stuhn**): to shock or daze someone or something

Comprehension Questions

1. Can you name three parts of an ant?
2. Can you name three kinds of ants?
3. Can you share three ways that ants cooperate?
4. Can you share three more fantastic facts about ants?

Bonus Fast Facts

- Ants have lived on Earth for more than 100 million years.
- Some ants have wings.
- Some ants can sting.
- Ants are closely related to wasps and bees.